THE STORY OF THE ACTION

Aïda, daughter of Amonasro, King of Ethiopia, has been led into captivity by the Egyptians. While in bondage sne conceives a tender passion for Radames, a young Egyptian warrior, who warmly responds to her affection. The opening incidents of the opera disclose these facts, and set forth, besides, the choice of Radames as leader of an expedition against the invading forces of Ethiopia, and the love, still unrevealed, of Amneris, daughter of Egypt's sovereign, for the fortune-favored chieftain. Amneris suspects the existence of a rival, but does not learn the truth until Radames returns victorious. The second act commences with a scene between the Princess and the slave. Amneris wrests from Aïda the secret she longs and yet dreads to fathom, and dire hate at once possesses her. Radames comes back, laden with spoils. Among his prisoners—his rank being unknown to his captors—is Amonasro, father of Aïda. Radames asks of his sovereign that the captives be freed. The King consents to releasing all of them except Aïda and Amonasro. The monarch then bestows upon the unwilling Radames the hand of Amneris, and amid songs of jubilation the act terminates. In the third act the marriage of Amneris and Radames is on the eve of celebration. Radames, however, is devotedly attached to Aïda, and the maiden, urged thereunto by Amonasro, seeks to persuade the soldier to flee to Ethiopia and turn his sword against his native land. Without resolving upon the act of treachery, Radames lends an ear to her supplications. The party is about to take to flight, when the High Priest, Ramphis, and Amneris, both of whom have overheard the lovers, appear. Aïda and Amonasro, on the advice of Radames, escape. Radames remains to await his fate. This is speedily decided. Radames, in act the fourth, is tried on a charge of treason. Amneris, repentant, vainly endeavors to save his life,—for the lover of Aïda scorns to renounce her,—and he is deaf to the entreaties of the daughter of the King, whose jealousy, as Amneris herself is aware, has brought about his downfall. The dénouement is not long delayed. The final picture shows the interior of the Temple of Vulcan. Above is the hall of worship; below, the vault in which Radames, doomed to die, is interred alive by the priests. As the stone is sealed over his head, Aïda, who has awaited Radames in the tomb, rises before him. The lovers are locked in a last embrace as Amneris, heart-broken, kneels in prayer on the marble which parts from the living the couple now united in death.

CHARACTERS

AÏDA, an Ethiopian Slave . . . . Soprano

AMNERIS, Daughter of the King of Egypt . . . . Mezzo Soprano

RADAMES, Captain of the Guard . . . . Tenor

AMONASRO, King of Ethiopia, Father of Aïda . . . . Baritone

RAMPHIS, High Priest . . . . Bass

THE KING OF EGYPT . . . . Bass

A MESSENGER . . . . Tenor

Priests, Priestesses, Soldiers, Ethiopian Slaves and Prisoners, Egyptians, Etc.

Scene: Memphis and Thebes, during the Epoch of the Pharaohs.

AÏDA

OPERA IN FOUR ACTS

Book by
A. GHISLANZONI

Music by
GIUSEPPE VERDI

WILDSIDE PRESS

NOTE

The opera of "Aïda" was written at the request of the Khedive of Egypt, Ismail Pacha, for the new opera house which he had built in Cairo. Contrary to the general impression, "Aïda" was not written for the opening of the opera house which took place in 1869. The first performance did take place there, however, but not until December 24, 1871; and the first performance in Europe was at the La Scala, Milan, February 8, 1872.

AÏDA

ACT I.

SCENE I.—Hall in the Palace of the King at Memphis; to the right and left a colonnade with statues and flowering shrubs; at the back a grand gate, from which may be seen the temples and palaces of Memphis and the Pyramids.

(RADAMES and RAMPHIS.)

Ramphis.

Yes, a report runs that the Ethiopian dares
Again defy us, and the Valley of the Nile
And Thebes to threaten.—A messenger shortly
Will bring the truth.

Radames.

The sacred Isis
Didst thou consult?

Ramphis.

She has named
Of the Egyptian phalanxes
The supreme leader.

Radames.

Oh! happy man!

Ramphis

(with meaning, gazing at RADAMES).

Young and brave is he. Now to the king
I convey the decrees of the goddess.

(Exit.)

Radames

(alone).

If that warrior I were! If my dream
Should be verified! An army of brave men
Led by me—victory—the applause
Of all Memphis! And to thee, my sweet Aïda,
To return, crowned with laurels!
To say to thee,—for thee I have fought, and for thee conquered!

ATTO I.

SCENA I.—Sala nel Palazza del Re a Menfi. A destra e a sinistra una colonnata con statue e arbusti in flori—Grande porta nel fondo, de cui appariccone i tempii, i palazzi di Menfi e le Piramidi.

(RADAMES e RAMFIS.)

Ramfis.

Sì: corre voce che l'Etiope ardisca
Sfidarci ancora, e del Nilo la valle
E Tebe miniacciar—Fra breve un messo
Recherà il ver.

Radames.

La sacra
Iside consultasti?

Ramfis.

Ella ha nomato
Delle Egizie falangi
El condottier supremo.

Radames.

Oh lui felice!

Ramfis

(con intenzione, fissando RADAMES).

Giovine e prode è desso—Ora, del Nume
Reco i decreti al Re.

(Esce.)

Radames

(solo).

Se quel guerrier
Io fossi! se il mio sogno
Si avverasse!... Un esercito di prodi
Da me guidato... e la vittoria... e il plauso
Di Menfi tutta!—E a te, mia dolce Aïda,
Tornar di lauri cinto...
Dirti: per te ho pugnato e per te ho vinto!

CELESTE AÏDA—*RADIANT AÏDA*   Air (Radames)

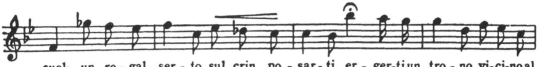

suol; un re - gal ser - to sul crin po - sar - ti, er - ger-ti un tro - no vi - ci-no al
land, Gar-lands im - pe - rial I would wreathe o'er thee, Raise thee a throne e - ter-nal to

sol, un tro - no vi - ci-no al sol, un tro - no vi - ci-no al sol. —
stand; A throne near the sun to stand, A throne near the sun to stand. —

Amneris.   (Enter AMNERIS.)

    What unwonted fire in thy glance!
    With what noble pride glows thy face.
    Worthy of envy—oh, how much—
    Would be the woman whose beloved aspect
    Should awaken in thee this light of joy!

Radames.

    With an adventurous dream
    My heart was blessed. To-day the goddess
    Declared the name of the warrior who to the
      field
    The Egyptian troops shall lead. If I were
    To such honor destined!

Amneris.

    Has not another dream
    More gentle, more sweet,
    Spoken to thy heart? Hast thou not in
      Memphis
    Desires—hopes?

Radames.

    I! (What a question!
    Perhaps—the hidden love
    Which burns my heart she has discovered—
    The name of her slave
    She reads in my thoughts!)

Amneris.

    (Oh! woe if another love
    Should burn in his heart;
    Woe, if my search should penetrate
    This fatal mystery!)

                  (Enter AÏDA.)

Radames   (seeing AÏDA).

    She!

Amneris.   (AMNERIS e detto.)

    Quale insolita givia
    Nel tuo sguardo! Di quale
    Nobil fierezza ti balena il volto!
    Degna di invidia oh! quanto
    Saria la donna il cui bramato aspetto
    Tanta luce di gaudio in te destasse!

Radames.

    D'un sogno avventuroso
    Si beava il mio cuore—Oggi, la diva
    Profferse il nome del guerrier che al campo
    Le schìere Egizie condurrà... S'io fossi
    A tale onor prescelto...

Amneris.

    Nè un altro sogno mai
    Più gentil... più soave...
    Al cuore ti parlò?... Non hai tu in Menfi
    Desiderii... speranze?

Radames.

    Io!... (quale inchiesta!)
    Forse... l'arcano amore
    Scoprì che m' arde in core...
    Della sua schiava il nome
    Mi lesse nel pensier!)

Amneris.

    (Oh! guai se un altro amore
    Ardesse a lui nel core!...
    Guai se il mio sguardo penetra
    Questo fatal mister!)

                (AÏDA e detto.)

Radames   (vedendo AÏDA).

    Dessa!

Amneris.

(He is moved! And what
A glance he turns to her!
Aïda!—My rival—
Perhaps is she?)

(After a short silence turning to AIDA.)

Amneris.

(Ei si turba... e quale
Sguardo rivolse a lei!
Aïda!... a me rivale...
Forse saria costei?)

(Dopo breve silenzio volgendois ad AIDA.)

6   VIENI, O DILETTA—*COME, DEAREST FRIEND*   Trio (Amneris, Aïda and Radames)

Andante mosso

Vie_ ni o di - let - ta ap-pres-sa-ti   schia - va non sei ne an-
Come, dear-est friend, come near to me,   Slave_ I no long-er

cel - la,   Qui_ do-ve in dol - ce fa - - sci-no   Io ti chia-mai so -
name_ thee;   Here_ in af - fec - tion's ten - - der bonds,   My sis-ter I pro-

rel - la   Pian - gi?   del-le tue la - cri-me sve - la il se -
claim thee,   Weep'st thou?   Why are these tears flow-ing, tell me thy

AIDA *Più mosso*

gre - to, _ sve-la il se - gre-to a me. Ohi-mè!   di guer-ra fre - me-re   l'a-
se - cret,_ thy se-cret tell to me. A-las!   the din of strife re-sounds, The

tro - ce gri-do io sen - to   Per l'in-fe-li - ce pa-tri-a,   per me,   per voi pa-
war- like hosts as - sem-ble,   For my un-hap- py na-tive land, For me,   for thee, I

AMN

ven - to.   Fa-vel-li il ver?   nè s'a-gi-ta più gra-ve cu-ra in te?
trem - ble.   Dost tru-ly speak?   no grav-er care dis-turbs thy gen-tle heart?

Allegro   RADAMES

Tre-ma,   o re - a schia-va,   Nel vel-
*Trem-ble,   O slave dis- sem-bling!   Up - on_*

ra - to a-mor è___ pian-to di___ sven-tu - ra - - - to a-mor.
hap - py smart, Are flow-ing from love's un - hap - - - py smart!

(Enter the KING, preceded by his Guards and followed by RAMPHIS, his Ministers, Priests, Captains, etc., etc. An Officer of the Palace, and afterwards a Messenger.)

King.
Great cause summons you,
O faithful Egyptians, around your king.
From the confines of Ethiopia a Messenger
Just now arrived—grave news he brings.
Be pleased to hear him.
(To an Officer.)
Let the messenger come forward.

Messenger.
The sacred soil of Egypt is invaded
By the barbarous Ethiopians! Our fields
Are devastated! The crops burned!
And emboldened by the easy victory, the depredators
Already march on Thebes.

All.
They dare so much!

Messenger.
A warrior indomitable and fierce
Conducts them—Amonasro.

All.
The King!

Aïda.
(My father!)

Messenger.
Already Thebes is in arms, and from the hundred gates
Breaks forth upon the invading barbarian,
Carrying war and death.

King.
Yes, be war and death our cry!

All.
War! War!

King.
Tremendous! inexorable!
(Addressing RADAMES.)
Of our unconquered legions
Venerated Isis

(Il RE, preceduto dalle sue guardie e seguito da RAMFIS da Ministri, Sacerdoti, Capitani, ecc., ecc. Un Uffiziale di Palazzo, indi un Messaggiero.)

Il Re.
Alta cagion vi aduna,
O fidi Egizii, al vostro Re d'intorno.
Dal confin d'Etiópia un Messaggiero
Dianzi giungea—gravi novelle ei reca...
Vi piaccia udirlo...
(Ad un Ufficiale.)
Il Messaggier si avanzi!

Messaggiero.
Il sacro suolo dell' Egitto è invaso
Dai barbari Etiope—i nostri campi
Fur devastati... arse le messi... e baldi
Della facil vittoria, i predatori
Già marciano su Tebe...

Tutti.
Ed osan tanto!

Messaggiero.
Un guerriero indomabile, feroce,
Li conduce—Amonasro.

Tutti.
Il Re!

Aïda.
(Mio padre!)

Messaggiero.
Già Tebe è in armi e dalle cento porte
Sul barbaro invasore
Proromperà, guerra recando e morte.

Il Re.
Si: guerra e morte il nostro grido sia.

Tutti.
Guerra! guerra!

Il Re.
Tramenda, inesorata...
(Accostandosi a RADAMES.)
Iside venerata
Di nostre schiere invitte

Has already designated the supreme leader—
Radames.

All.

Radames!

Radames.

Thanks be to the gods!
My prayers are answered.

Amneris.

(He leader!)

Aïda.

(I tremble!)

King.

Now move, O warrior,
To the temple of Vulcan. Gird thee
With the sacred arms, and fly to victory.
Up! To the sacred bank of the Nile
Hasten, Egyptian heroes;
From every heart let burst the cry,
War and death to the foreigner!

Ramphis and Priests.

Glory to the gods! Remember all
That they rule events;
That in the power of the gods alone
Lies the fate of warriors.

Ministers and Captains.

Up! Of the Nile's sacred shore
Be our breasts the barrier;
Let but one cry resound:
War and death to the foreigner!

Radames.

Holy rage of glory
Fills all my soul.
Up! Let us rush to victory:
War and death to the foreigner!

Amneris

(bringing a banner and consigning it to RADAMES).
From my hand receive, O leader,
The glorious standard.
Be it thy guide, be it thy light,
On the path of glory.

Aïda.

(For whom do I weep? For whom pray?
What power binds me to him!
I must love him! And this man
Is an enemy—an alien!)

Già designava il condottier supremo:
Radames.

Tutti.

Radames.

Radames.

Sien grazie ai Numi!
I miei voti fur paghi.

Amneris.

(Ei duce!)

Aïda.

(Io tremo!)

Il Re.

Or, di Vulcano al tempio
Muovi, o guerrier—Le sacre
Armi ti cingi e alla vittoria vola.
Su! del Nilo al sacro lido
Accorrete, Egizii eroi;
Da ogni cor prorompa il grido.
Guerra e morte allo stranier!

Ramfis e Sacerdoti.

Gloria ai Numi! ognun rammenti
Ch'essi reggono gli eventi—
Che in poter d'e Numi solo
Stan le sorti guerrier.

Ministri e Capitani.

Su! del Nilo al sacro lido
Sien barriera i nostri petti;
Non echeggi che un sol grido:
Guerra e morte allo stranier!

Radames.

Sacro fremito di gloria
Tutta l'anima mi investe—
Su! corriamo alla vittoria!
Guerra e morte allo stranier!

Amneris

(recando una bandiera e consegnandota a RADAMES).
Di mia man ricevi, o duce,
Il vessillo glorioso;
Ti sia guida, ti sia luce
Della gloria sul sentier.

Aïda.

(Per chi piango? per chi prego?...
Qual poter m'avvince a lui!
Deggio amarlo... ed è costui
Un nemico... uno stranier!)

All.

> War! War! Extermination to the invader!
> Go, Radames, return conqueror!
>> (Exeunt all but AÏDA.)

10 *Aïda.*

> Return victorious! And from thy lips
> Went forth the impious word! Conqueror
> Of my father—of him who takes arms
> For me—to give me again
> A country, a kingdom; and the illustrious
>   name
> Which here I am forced to conceal! Con-
>   queror
> Of my brothers, with whose dear blood
> I see him stained, triumphant in the ap-
>   plause
> Of the Egyptian hosts; and behind the
>   chariot
> A king!—my father—bound with chains!
> The insane word
> Forget, O gods!
> Return the daughter
> To the bosom of her father;
> Destroy the squadrons
> Of our oppressors!
> Unhappy one! What did I say?—And my
>   love
> Can I ever forget,
> This fervid love which oppresses and en-
>   slaves,
> As the sun's ray which now blesses me?
> Shall I call death
> On Radames?—On him whom I love so
>   much?
> Ah! Never on earth was heart torn
> By more cruel agonies.
> The sacred names of father, of lover,
> I can neither utter, nor remember—
> For the one—for the other—confused—
>   trembling—
> I would weep—I would pray;
> But my prayer changes to blasphemy.
> My tears are a crime—my sighs a wrong—
> In dense night the mind is lost—
> And in the cruel anguish I would die.

Tutti.

> Guerra! guerra! sterminio all' invasor!
> Va, Radames, ritorna vincitor!
>> (Escono tutti meno AÏDA.)

Aïda.

> Ritorna vincitor!... E dal mio labbro
> Uscì liempi parola!—Vincitore
> Del padre mio... di lui che impugna l'armi
> Per me... per ridonarmi
> Una patria, una reggia! e il nome illustre
> Che qui celar mie è forza—Vincitore
> De' miei fratelli... ond' io lol vegga, tinto
> Del sangue amato, trionfar nel plauso
> Dell' Egizie coorti!... E dietro il carro,
> Un Re... mio padre... di catene avvinto!...
>
> L'insana parola,
> O Numi, sperdete!
> Al seno d'un padre
> La figlia rendete;
> Struggete le squadre
> Dei nostri oppressor!
> Sventurata! che dissi?... e l'amor mio?...
> Dunque scordar poss' io
> Questo fervido amor che oppressa e schiava
> Come raggio di sol qui mi beava?
> Imprecherò la morte
> A Radames... a lui che amo pur tanto!
> Ah! non fu in terra mai
> Da più crudeli angoscie un core affranto.
> I sacri nomi di padre... di amante
> Nè profferir poss' lo, nè ricordar...
> Per l'un... per l'altro... confusa... tremante...
> Io piangere vorrei... vorrei pregar.
> Ma la mia prece inbestemmia si muta...
> Delitto è il pianto a me... colna il sospir...
> In notte cupa la mente è perduta...
> E nell' ansia crudel vorrei morir.

NUMI, PIETÀ!—*PITY, KIND HEAVEN*   Air (Aïda)

Nu-mi, pie - tà— Del mio sof-frir! Spe-me— non v'ha pel mio do-
Pi - ty, kind Heav'n, To Thee I fly; Hope there is none in this my

lor. A - mor fa - tal, Tre - men-do a - mor Spez - za— mi il
woe. Oh! fa - tal love, Thy pow'r I know, Break thou, my

cor,— fam-mi mò - rir! Nu - mi,— pie - tà del mio— sof-
heart,— cause me to die. Pi - ty,— kind Heav'n, Thy pow'r I

frir, Ah!— pie - tà, Nu-mi,pie - tà,— del mio— sof - frir,— Nu-mi, pie-
know. Oh,— kind Heav'n, pi-ty my woe, Thy mer - cy show,— pi-ty, kind

tà del mio— sof - frir, pie - tà, pie - tà, del mio sof - frir
Heav'n, re - lieve— my— woe: re - lieve my woe, re - lieve my woe.

SCENE II.—Interior of the Temple of Vulcan at Memphis. A mysterious light descends from above; a long row of columns one behind another is lost in the darkness; Statues of various deities; in the middle of the scene, above a platform covered with carpet, rises the altar, surmounted by sacred emblems; from golden tripods rises the smoke of incense.

PRIESTS and PRIESTESSES—RAMPHIS at the foot of the altar, afterwards RADAMES—The song of the PRIESTESSES accompanied by harps, is heard from the interior.

Priestesses   (in the interior).

Infinite Phthah, of the world
Animating spirit,
We invoke thee!

Infinite Phthah, of the world
The fructifying spirit,
We invoke thee!

SCENA II.—Interno del Tempio di Vulcano a Menfi. Una luce misteriosa scende dal' alto.—Uno lunga fila di colonne l'una all' altra addossate, si perde fra le tenebre. Statue di varie Divinità. Nel mezzo della scena, sovra un palco coperto da tappeti, sorge l'altare sormontato da emblemi sacri. Dai tripedi d'oro si innalza il fumo degli incensi.

SACERDOTI e SACERDOTESSE—RAMFIS ai piedi dell' altare—A suo tempo, RADAMES—Si sente dall' interno il canto delle SACERDOTESSE accompagnato dalle arpe.

Sacerdotesse   (nell' interno).

Immenso Fthà, del mondo
Spirito animator,
Noi ti invochiamo!

Immenso Fthà, del mondo
Spirito fecondator,
Noi ti invochiamo!

Fire uncreate, eternal,
Whence the sun has light,
We invoke thee!

Fuoco increato, eterno,
Onde ebbe luce il sol,
Noi ti invochiamo!

Priests.

Thou who from nothing hast made
The waters, the earth and the heavens,
We invoke thee!

God, who of thy spirit
Art son and father,
We invoke thee!

Life of the Universe
Gift of eternal love,
We invoke thee.

Sacerdoti.

Tu che dal nulla hai tratto
L'onde, la terra e il ciel,
Noi ti invochiamo!

Nume che del tuo spirito
Sei figlio e genitor,
Noi ti invochiamo!

Vita dell' Universo,
Mito di eterno amor,
Noi ti invochiamo!

(Enter RADAMES, introduced unarmed—While he goes to the altar the PRIESTESSES execute the sacred dance—On the head of RADAMES is placed a silver veil.)

(RADAMES viene introdotto senz' armi—Montre va all' altare, le SACERDOTESSE eseguiscono la danza sacra—Sul capo di RADAMES vien steso un velo d'argento.)

Ramphis.

Mortal, beloved of the gods, to thee
Is confided the fate of Egypt. Let the holy
   sword
Tempered by the gods, in thy hand become
To the enemy, terror—a thunderbolt—
   death.
      (Turning himself to the gods.)
God, guardian and avenger
Of this sacred land,
Spread thy hand
Over the Egyptian soil.

Ramfis.

Mortal, diletto ai Numi—A te fidate
Son d'Egitto le sorti,—Il sacro brando
Dal Dio temprato, per tua man diventi
Ai nemici terror, folgore, morte.
      (Volgendozi al Nume.)
Nume, custode e vindice
Di questa sacra terra,
La mano tua distendi
Sovra l'Egizio suol.

Radames.

God, who art leader and arbiter
Of every human war,
Protect thou and defend
The sacred soil of Egypt.

Radames.

Nume, che duce ed arbitro
Sei d'ogni umana guerra,
Proteggi tu, difendi
D'Egitto il sacro suol!

(While RADAMES is being invested with the consecrated armor, the PRIESTS and PRIESTESSES resume the religious hymn and mystic dance.)

(Mentre RADAMES viene investito delle armi sacre, le SACERDOTESSE e SACERDOTI riprendono l'inno religioso e la mistica danza.)

END OF THE FIRST ACT.

FINE DELL' ATTO PRIMO.

14

ACT II.

SCENE I.

A Hall in the Apartments of Amneris.

Amneris surrounded by female Slaves, who are adorning her for the triumphal festival. From tripods arise aromatic perfumes. Moorish Slave Boys dancing and agitating feather fans.

Slave Girls.

Thou who amidst hymns and plaudits
Raisest thy flight to glory
Terrible even as a god!
Effulgent as the sun,
Come, on thy tresses rain
Laurels and flowers interwoven;
Let sound the songs of glory
With the songs of love.

Amneris.

(Come, my love, intoxicate me;
Make my heart blessed!)

Slave Girls.

Now where are the barbarian
Hordes of the foreigner?
Like a mist they scatter
At the breath of the warrior.
Come: gather the reward
Of glory, O conqueror;
Victory smiled upon thee—
Love shall smile upon thee.

Amneris.

(Come, my love, revive me
Again with thy dear voice!)
Silence! Aïda approaches us;
Daughter of the vanquished, her grief to me
is sacred.

(At a sign from Amneris all withdraw to a distance.)

In seeing her again, the fearful doubt
Awakens itself within me.
Let the fatal mystery be at last rent.

(Enter Aïda.)

Amneris

(to Aïda, with feigned affection).

The fate of arms was deadly to thy people,
Poor Aïda. The grief
Which weighs down thy heart I share with
thee.
I am thy friend:
Thou shalt have all from me—thou shalt live
happy.

ATTO II.

SCENA I.

Una Sala nell' Appartmento di Amneris.

Amneris circondata dalle Schiave che li abbigliano per la festa trionfale. Dai tripodi si eleva il profumo degli aromi. Giovani schiavi mori denzando agitano i ventagli di piume.

Schiave.

Chi mai fra gli inni e i plausi
Erge alla gloria il vol,
Al par di un Dio terribile,
Fulgente al par del sol?
Vieni; sul crin ti piovano
Conteste ai lauri i fior;
Suonin di gloria i cantici
Coi cantici d'amor

Amneris.

(Vieni, amor mio, mi inebria...
Fammi beato il cor!)

Schiave.

Or, dove son le barbare
Orde dello stranier?
Siccome nebbia sparvero
Al soffio del guerrier.
Vieni: di gloria il premio
Raccogli, o vincitor;
T'arrise la vittoria,
T'arriderà l'amor.

Amneris.

(Vieni, amor mio, ravvivami
D'un caro accento ancor!)
Silenzio! Aïda verso noi si avanza...
Figlia dei vinti, il suo dolor mi è sacro.

(Ad un cenno di Amneris tutti allontanano.)

Nel rivederla, il dubbio
Atroce in me si desta...
Il mistero fatal si squarci alfine!

(Amneris ed Aïda.)

Amneris

(ad Aïda con simulata amorevolezza).

Fu la sorte dell' armi a' tuoi funesta,
Povera Aïda!—Il lutto
Che ti pesa sul cor teco divido.
Io son l'amica tua...
Tutto da me tu avrai—vivrai felice!

Aïda.

    Can I be happy,

    Far from my native land; here where un-
      known

    To me is the fate of father and brothers?

Amneris.

    Deeply do I pity thee! Nevertheless they
      have an end,

    The ills of this world. Time will heal

    The anguish of thy heart.

    And more than time—a powerful god—love.

Aïda.

    Felice esser poss' io

    Lungi dal suol natio... qui dove ignota

    M'è la sorte del padre e dei fratelli?

Amneris.

    Ben ti compiango; pure hanno un confine

    I mali di quaggiù... Sanerà il tempo

    Le angosce del tuo core...

    E più che il tempo, un Dio possente...

    Amore.

AMORE, AMORE!—*O LOVE IMMORTAL!*　Duet (Aïda and Amneris)

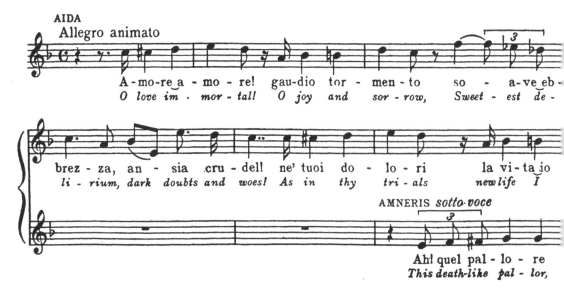

ri - so mi__ schiu-de il ciel,___ Ne' tuoi do - lo-ri la vi-ta io
rap - ture thy__ smiles dis - close,___ As in thy tri-als new life I

D'in-ter-ro-gar-la qua-si hò sgo-men-to,
Her will I ques-tion— feign-ing com-mo-tion,

sen - to un tuo sor - ri - so mi schiu-de il ciel.
bor - row, A heav'n of rap-ture thy smiles dis - close.

Di-vi - do l'an-sie del su - - o ter-ror.
As if her trou-ble to share___ or re - move.

AMNERIS

Eb-ben qual nuo - vo fer-mi-to t'as-sai, gen-til A - ï - da?
What new a - larm dis - turbs thee now, my gen-tle friend, A - ï - da?

I tuoi se - gre - ti sve-la-mi, al - l'a - mor mi - o, al - l'a-mor mio t'af-
Thy se-cret thoughts un-veil to me, trust my__ af - fec-tion, to my fond love con-

fi - da, Tra i for-ti che pu - gna-ro-no del-la tua pa-tria a dan-ne, quel-
fide thee! A-mong the braves who fought so well, lost in their coun-try's ser-vice, Has

AIDA

cu - no un dol-ce af-fan-no for - se a te in cor de-stò? Che
some one a ten-der sor-row hap - ly wak-en'd in your heart? What

AMNERIS

par-li? A tut-ti— bar-ba-ra non si mos-trò la sor-te Se in cam-po il dul-ce im-
say'st thou? To all the— fates have not so cru-el - ly in - tend-ed. If on the field the

AIDA

pa - vi-do cad-de tra-fit-tò a mor-te Che-mai di-ce-sti! mi - se-ra!
lead- er brave doth fall, by death ex - tend - ed, What art thou say-ing! Hap - less me!

2

mi - se-ra!   Per sem-pre io pian-ge-ró!   Av-ver-si
Hap - less me!   My tears shall for ev - er flow!   The gods have

AMN.

sem-pre a me fu - rò i Nu-mi Tre - ma! in cor ti les-si tu
ev - er from child- hood op - posed me. Trem - ble! I read thy se-cret, thou

AIDA   **AMN.**

l'a - mi!   I - o! Non men-ti - re!   Un det-to an-co-ra e il ve-ro sa-
lov'st him!   Love him! Lie no long-er!   Yet one word fur-ther, the truth I wil

f a piacere   **AIDA**

prò, Fis-sa mi in vol-to io t'in-gan-na-va Ra-dam-es vi-ve! Vi-
know, Look firm-ly on me, I have de-ceived thee; Ra-dam-es liv-eth! Liv-

AMN

- ve! ah gra-zie, o Nu-mi! E an-cor— men-tir tu spe-ri? Si, tu
- *eth! thanks, kind Heav-en! And still— to lie thou'rt read-y? Yes, thou*

l'a - mi_ Ma l'a-mo an-ch'io in-ten-di tu? son tua ri-
*lov'st him_* *I love him too, dost thou not hear? I am thy*

val-le fi - glia de' Fa - ra - o - ni Mia ri-va-le! eb-ben sia
ri-val, daugh - - ter of kings E - gyp-tian, Thou my ri-val! 'tis well, so

pu - re An-ch'io son tal Ah! Che dis - si mai? pie-
be it! And I am too_ Ah! What have I said? for-

Adagio

tà! per - do-no! Ah!_____ pie-tà! ti pren-da del mio do-
give, and pit - y, Ah!_____ Let this my) sor-row thy warm heart

lor! È ve-ro, io l'a-mo d'im-men-so a-mor. Tu sei fe - li-ce, tu sei pos-
move. 'Tis true I a-dore him with bound-less love. Thou art so hap-py, thou art so

sen - te io_ vi - vo so - lo_ per que-sto a-mor! Tre - ma, vil
might - y, I_ can - not live hence from love a - part! Trem - ble, vile

schia - va! spez-za il tuo co-re! Se - gnar tuo mor - te, pùo quest'a-
min - ion! be_ ye heart-bro-ken, War-rant of death_ this love shall be-

mo - re, Del tuo des-ti - no ar-bi-tra so-no,d'o-dio e ven-det - ta le fur-ie hò in

to - ken,What may thy fate be, I am judge on-ly, Ha-tred and ven-geance hold sway in my

cor. Tu sei fe- -li-ce, tu sei pos - sen - te, io_ vi-vo

heart. Thou art so hap-py, thou art so might - y, I_ can-not

so - lo_ per quest'a - mor! Pie-tà! pie-tà! ti pren - da del mio do -

live hence from love a - part! For-give! for-give! Let sor - -row thy warm heart

lor! pie-tà! pie - tà! ti pren - da dal mi - o_ do-lor.

move, for-give! for - give! Let pit - -y find place in_thy heart!

Amneris.

Ah, the pomp which approaches,
With me, O slave, thou shalt assist;
Thou prostrate in the dust—
I on the throne beside the King;
Come, follow me, and thou shalt learn
If thou canst contend with me.

Aïda.

Ah, pity! What more remains to me?
My life is a desert;
Live and reign, thy rage
I will quickly appease.
This love which angers thee
In the tomb I will extinguish.

SCENE II.

An entrance to the City of Thebes. In front a group of palms; to the right the Temple of Ammon; to the left a throne surmounted by a purple canopy; at the back a triumphal gate. The scene is crowded with people.
Enter the KING, followed by Ministers, Priests, Captains, Fan-Bearers, Ensign-Bearers, etc., etc. Afterwards AMNERIS with AÏDA and SLAVES. The KING seats himself on the throne; AMNERIS places herself to the left of the KING.

People.

Glory to Egypt, and to Isis,
Who the sacred soil protects;

Amneris.

Alla pompa che si appresta,
Meco, o schiava, assisterai;
Tu prostrata nella polvere,
Io sul trono, accanto al Re.
Vien... mi segui... e apprenderai
Se lottar tu puoi con me.

Aïda.

Ah! pietà!... che più mi resta?
Un deserto è la mia vita:
Vivi e regna, il tuo furore
Io tra breve placherò.
Questo amore che ti irrita
Nella tomba spegnerò.

SCENA II.

Uno degli ingressi della Città di Tebe. Sul davanti un gruppo di palme; a destra il Tempio di Ammone; a sinistra un trono sormontato da un baldacchino di porpora; nel fondo una porta trionfale; la scena è ingombra di popolo.
Entra il RE, seguito dai Ministri, Sacerdoti, Capitani, Flabelliferi, Porta-Insegne, ecc., ecc. Quindi AMNERIS con AÏDA e SCHIAVE. Il Re va a sedere sul trono. AMNERIS prende posto alla sinistra del RE.

Popolo.

Gloria all Egitto e ad Iside
Che il sacro suol protegge;

To the king who rules the Delta
Festal hymns let us raise.
Come, O champion warrior,
Come to rejoice with us;
In the path of the heroes,
Laurels and flowers let us **strew.**

Women.

Weave the lotus with the laurel
On the hair of the conqueror
A sweet shower of the flowers,
Spread on their arms a veil.
Let us dance, daughters of **Egypt,**
The mystic dances,
As around the sun
Dance the stars of heaven!

Priests.

To the supreme arbiters of **victory**
Raise your eyes;
Render thanks to the gods
On the happy day.
Thus for us with glory
May the future be **marked,**
Nor may that fate seize us
That struck the barbarians.

(The Egyptian troops, preceded by trumpets, defile before the KING—the chariots of war follow—the ensigns—the sacred vases and statues of the gods—troops of Dancing GIRLS who carry the treasures of the defeated—and lastly RADAMES, under a canopy borne by twelve Officers.)

King

(who descends from the throne to embrace RADAMES).

Saviour of thy country, I salute thee.
Come, and let my daughter with her own
    hand
Place upon you the triumphal crown.

(RADAMES bows before AMNERIS, who places the crown upon him.)

King

(to RADAMES).

Now ask of me
What thou most wishest. Nothing denied
    to thee
On such a day shall be—I swear it
By my crown, by the sacred gods.

Radames.

Deign first to let the prisoners
Be drawn up before thee.

(Enter between the Guards the Ethiopian prisoners, AMONASRO last. dressed as an Officer.)

Al Re che il Delta ragge
Inni festosi alziam!
Vieni, o guerriero vindice,
Vieni a gioir con noi;
Sul passo degli eroi
I lauri e i fior versiam!

Donne.

S'intrecci il loto al lauro
Sul crin dei vincitori;
Nembo gentil di fiori
Stenda sull' armi un vel.
Danziam, fanciulle Egizie,
Le mistiche carole,
Come d'intorno al sole
Donzano gli astri in ciel!

Sacerdoti.

Della vittoria agli arbitri
Supremi il guarde ergete;
Grazie agli Dei rendete
Nel forsunato di.
Così per noi di gloria
Sia l'avvenir segnato,
Nè mai ci colga il fato *Disc 2*
Che i barbari colpi.

(Le truppe Egizie precedute dalle fanfare sfilano dinanze al RE—Seguono i carri di guerra, le insegne i vasi sacri, le statue degli Dei—Un drapello di danzatrici che recano i tesori dei vinti—Da ultimo, RADAMES, sotto un baldacchino portato da dodici Ufficiali.)

Il Re

(che scende dal trono per abbracciare RADAMES).

Salvator della patria, io ti saluto.
Vieni, e mia figlia di sua man ti porga
Il serto trionfale.

(RADAMES si inchina davanti AMNERIS che gli porge la corona.)

Il Re

(a RADAMES).

Ora, a me chiedi
Quanto più brami. Nulla a te negato
Sarà in tal dì—lo giuro
Per la corono mia, pei sacri Numi.

Radames.

Concedi in pria che innanzi a te sien tratti
I prigionier...

Entrano fra le guardie i prigionieri Etiopi, ultimo, AMONASRO, vestito da Uffiziale.)

Aïda.

    What do I see? He!—my father!

All.

    Her father!

Amneris.

    In our power!

Aïda

              (embracing her father).

    Thou prisoner!

Amonasro

              (softly to AÏDA).

    Betray me not!

King

              (to AMONASRO).

    Draw thou near—

    Then—thou art?

Amonasro.

    Her father.—I also fought—

    Was conquered, and death I sought in vain.

    (Pointing to the uniform in which he is dressed.)

    This livery that I wear may tell you

    That I have defended my king and my coun-
        try.

    Fate was hostile to our arms;

    Vain was the courage of the brave.

    At my feet in the dust extended

    Lay the king, transfixed by many wounds;

    If the love of country is a crime

    We are all criminals—all ready to die!

    (Turning to the KING with a supplicating motion.)

    But thou, O king, thou puissant lord,

    Be merciful to those men.

    To-day we are stricken by Fate,

    To-morrow Fate may smite you.

Aïda, Prisoners and Female Slaves.

    Yes; by the gods we are stricken;

    Thy pity, thy mercy we implore;

    Ah! May you never have to suffer

    What is now given to us to suffer.

Ramphis and Priests.

    Destroy, O king, these savage hordes,

    Close your heart to their perfidious voices,

    By the gods they were doomed to death,

    Let the will of the gods be accomplished.

People.

    Priests, your anger soften,

Aïda.

    Che veggo?... Egli!... mia padre!

Tutti.

    Suo padre!

Amneris.

    In poter nostro!...

Aïda

              (abbracciando il padre).

    Tu! Prigionier!

Amneris

              (piano ad AÏDA).

    Non mi tradir!

Il Re

              (ad AMONASRO).

    Ti appressa...

    Dunque... tu sei?...

Amonasro.

    Suo padre—Anch' io pugnai...

    Vinti noi fummo e morte invancercai.

    (Accennando alla divisa che lo veste.)

    Questa assisa ch'io vesto vi dica

    Che il mio Re, la mia patria ho difeso:

    Fu la sorte a nostr' armi nemica...

    Tornò vano dei forti l'ardir.

    Al mio piè nella polve distesto

    Giacque il Re da più colpi traffito;

    Se l'amor della patria è delitto

    Siam rei tutti, siam pronti a morir!

    (Volgendosi al RE con accento supplichevole.)

    Ma tu, o Re, tu signore possente,

    A costoro ti volgi clemente...

    Oggi noi siam percossi dal fato

    Doman voi potria il fato colpir.

Aïda, Prigionieri e Schiava.

    Sî: dal Numi percossi non siamo;

    Tua pietà, tua clemenza imploriamo;

    Ah! giammai di soffrir vi sia dato

    Ciò che in oggi n'è dato soffrir!

Ramfis e Sacerdoti.

    Struggi, o Re, queste ciurme feroci,

    Chiudi il core alle perfide voci,

    Fur dai Numi votati alla morte,

    Si compisca dei Numi il voler!

Popolo.

    Sacerdoti, gli sdegni placate,

The humble prayer of the conquered hear,
And thou, O king, powerful and strong,
Open thy thoughts to mercy.

Radames
(fixing his eyes on AÏDA).

(The sorrow which speaks in that face
Renders it more beautiful to my sight;
Every drop of the beloved tears
Reanimates love in my breast.)

Amneris.

(What glances on her he turns!
With what flame their faces flash!
To such a fate as this am I destined?
Revenge groans in my heart.)

King.

Now that events smile favor upon us,
To these people let us show ourselves mer-
    ciful;
Pity ascends grateful to the gods,
And confirms the power of princes.

Radames
(to the KING).

O King! by the sacred gods,
By the splendor of thy crown,
Thou sworest to fulfill my vow?

King.

I swore.

Radames.

Well; of thee for the Ethiopian prisoners,
Life I demand and liberty.

Amneris.

(For all!)

Priests.

Death to the enemies of the country!

People.

Grace
For the unhappy.

Ramphis.

Listen, O King,
(To RADAMES.)
Even thou,
Young hero, listen to wise counsel:
They are enemies and they are warriors—
They have revenge in their hearts.
Emboldened by thy pardon
They will run to arms again.

L'umil prece dei vinti ascoltate;
E tu, o Re, tu possente, tu forte,
A clemenza dischiudi il pensier.

Radames
(fissando AÏDA).

(Il dolor che in quel volte favella
Al mio sguardo la rende più bella;
Ogni stilla del pianto adorato
Nel mio petto ravviva l'amor.)

Amneris

(Quali sguardi sovr' essa ha rivolti!
Di qual fiamma balenano i volti!
E a tal sorte serbata son io?...
La vendetta mi rugge nel cor.)

Il Re.

Or che fausti ne arridon gli eventi
A costoro mostriamci clementi:
La pietà sale ai Numi gradita
E rafferma dei Prenci il poter.

Radames
(al RE).

O Re: pei sacri Numi,
Per lo splendore della tua corona.
Compier giurasti il voto mio...

Il Re.

Giurai.

Radames.

Ebbene: a te pei prigionieri Etiopi
Vita domando e libertà.

Amneris.

(Per tutti!)

Sacerdoti.

Morte ai nemici della patria!

Popolo.

Grazie
Per gli infelici!

Ramfis.

Ascolta, o Re—
(A RADAMES.)
Tu pure
Giovine eroe, saggio consiglio ascolta:
Son nemici e prodi sono
La vendetta hanno nel cor,
Fatti audaci dal perdono
Correranno all' armi ancor!

Radames.

Amonasro, the warrior king slain,
No hope remains to the vanquished.

Ramphis.

At least
As an earnest of peace and security, among us
With her father let Aïda remain.
Let the rest be free.

King.

To thy counsel I yield.
Of security and peace a better pledge
I will now give: Radames, the country
Owes all to thee.   The hand of Amneris
Be thy reward.   Over Egypt one day
With her shalt thou reign.

Amneris.

(Now let the slave come—
Let her come to take my love from me—if
   she dares!)

King.

Glory to Egypt and to Isis,
Who the sacred soil defends,
Weave the lotus with the laurel
On the hair of the victors.

Priests.

Hymns let us raise to Isis,
Who the sacred soil defends;
Let us pray that the Fates may ever smile
Propitious on our country.

Aïda.

(What hope more remains to me?
To him glory and the throne.
To me, oblivion—the tears
Of hopeless love.)

Prisoners.

Glory to the merciful Egyptian
Who has unloosed our fetters,
Who restores us to the free
Paths of our native land!

Radames.

(The Thunder of the adverse gods
On my head descends—
Ah! no, the throne of Egypt
Is not worth the heart of Aïda.)

Radames.

Spento Amonasro il re guerrier, non resta
Speranza ai vinti.

Ramfis.

Almeno,
Arra di pace e securtà fra noi
Resti col padre Aïda...
Gli altri sien sciolti...

Il Re.

Al tuo consiglio io cedo.
Di securità, di pace un miglior pegno
Or io vuo' darvi—Radames, la patria
Tutto a te deve—D'Amneris la mano
Premio ti sia.   Sovra l'Egitto un giorno
Con essa regnerai...

Amneris.

(Venga or la schiava,
Venga a rapirmi l'amor mio... se l'osa!)

Il Re.

Gloria all' Egitto e ad Iside
Che il sacro suol difende,
S'intrecci il loto al lauro
Sul crin del vincitor!

Sacerdoti.

Inni leviamo ad Iside
Che il sacro suol difende;
Preghiam che i fati arridano
Fausti alla patria ognor.

Aïda.

(Qual speme omai più restami?
A lui la gloria e il trono...
A me l'oblio... le lacrime
Di disperato amor.)

Prigionieri

Gloria al clemente Egizio
Che i nostri ceppi ha sciolto,
Che ci ridona ai liberi
Solchi del patrio suol!

Radames.

(D'avverso Nume il folgore
Sul capo mio discende...
Ah no! d'Egitto il soglio
Non val d'Aïda il cor.)

Amneris.

> (By the unexpected joy
> I am intoxicated;
> All in one day are fulfilled
> The dreams of my heart.)

Amonasro (to AÏDA).

> Take heart, for thy country
> Expects happy events;
> For us the dawn of vengeance
> Is already near.

People.

> Glory to Egypt and to Isis,
> Who the sacred soil defends.
> Weave the lotus with the laurel
> On the hair of the victors!

END OF THE SECOND ACT.

Amneris.

> (Dall' inatteso giubilo
> Inebbriata io sono:
> Tutti in un dì si compiono
> I sogni del mio cor.)

Amonasro (ad AÏDA).

> Fa cor: della tua patria
> I lieti eventi aspetta;
> Per noi della vendetta
> Già prossimo è l'albor.

Popolo.

> Gloria all' Egitto e ad Iside
> Che il sacro suol difende!
> S'intrecci il loto al lauro
> Sul crin del vincitor!

FINE DELL' ATTO SECONDO.

ACT III.

SCENE.—The Banks of the Nile. Rocks of granite, among which grow palm trees; on the top of the rocks the Temple of Isis, half concealed among the foliage; it is starlight and bright moonlight.

Chorus (in the temple).

> O Thou who art of Osiris,
> Mother immortal and spouse,
> Goddess who awakenest the beatings
> In the heart of human creatures,
> Come piteous to our help,
> Mother of eternal love.

(From a boat, which approaches the shore, descend AM-NERIS, RAMPHIS, some Women closely veiled, and Guards.)

Ramphis (to AMNERIS)

> Come to the Temple of Isis.
> On the eve of thy nuptials implore
> The favor of the goddess. Isis rules
> The heart of mortals; every mystery
> Of mankind to her is known.

Amneris.

> Yes: I will pray that Radames may give me
> His whole heart, as mine to him
> Is consecrated forever.

Ramphis.

> Let us enter.
> Thou shalt pray till dawn. I shall be with thee.

(All enter the temple. The Chorus repeat the sacred song.)

ATTO III.

SCENA.—Le Rive del Nilo. Roccie di granito fra cui crescono dei palmizii. Sul vertice delle roccie il Templo d'Iside per metà nascosto tra le fronde. E notte stellata. Splendore di luna.

Coro (nel tempio).

> O tu che sei d'Osiride
> Madre immortale e sposa,
> Diva che i casti palpiti
> Desti agli amani in cor;
> Soccorri a noi pietosa,
> Madre d'eterno amor.

(Da una barca che approda alla riva, discendono AMNERIS, RAMFIS, alcune donne coperte da fitto velo e Guardie.)

Ramfis (ad AMNERIS).

> Vieni d'Iside al Tempio—alla vigilia
> Della tue nozze, implora
> Della Diva il favore—Iside legge
> Dei mortali nel cuore—ogni mistero
> Degli umani è a lei noto.

Amneris.

> Sì: pregherò che Radames mi doni
> Tutto il suo cor, come il mio core a lui
> Sacro è per sempre.

Ramfis.

> Pregherai fino all' alba—io sarò teco.

(Tutti entrano nel tempio. Il Coro ripete il canto sacro.)

Aïda

(entering cautiously, covered with a veil).

Here Radames will come. What would he
  say to me?
I tremble—ah, if thou comest
To give me, O cruel one, the last farewell,
The deep water of the Nile
Shall give me a tomb—and peace perhaps—
  and oblivion.

Aïda

(entra cautamente coperta da un velo).

Qui Radamès verrà... Che vorrà dirmi?
Io tremo... Ah! se tu vieni
A recarmi, o crudel, l'ultimo addio,
Del Nilo i cupi vortici
Mi daran tomba... e pace forse... e oblio.

OH! CIELI AZZURI—*O SKIES OF TENDER BLUE*   Air (Aïda)

q

Aïda.   (Enter Amonasro.)

Heaven! My father!

Amonasro.

Grave occasion
Leads me to thee, Aïda. **Nothing escapes**
My sight; thou art destroying thyself with
    love
For Radames. He loves thee, and here thou
    awaitest him,
The daughter of the Pharaohs is thy rival—
An infamous race, abhorred and fatal to us.

Aïda.

And I am in her power!—I, the daughter
Of Amonasro.

Amonasro.

In her power! No! If thou wishest,
This powerful rival thou shalt defeat,
And country, and throne, and love all shall
    be thine.
Thou shalt see again the balmy forests,
The fresh valleys, our temples of gold!

Aïda   (with transport).

I shall see again the balmy forests,
Our valleys, our temples of gold!

Amonasro.

Happy bride of him whom thou lovest so
    much,
Great jubilee thence shall be thine.

Aïda   (with transport).

One day only of such sweet enchantment,
One hour of such joy—and then to die!

Amonasro.

Nevertheless thou rememberest that the
    merciless Egyptian
Profaned our houses, temples, and altars;
He drew in fetters the ravished virgins—
Mothers, old men and children he has slain.

Aïda.

Ah! well I remember those unhappy days.
I remember the grief that my heart suffered.
Ah! make return to us, O gods,
The longed-for dawn of peaceful days.

Amonasro.

Delay not. In arms now are roused
Our people—everything is ready—

Aïda.   (Amonasro e Aïda.)

Cielo! mio padre!

Amonasro.

A te grave cagione
Mi adduce, Aïda. Nulla sfugge al mio
Sguardo—D'amor ti struggi
Per Radames... ei t'ama... e qui lo attendi
Dei Faraon la figlia è tua rivale...
Razza infame, aborrita e a noi fatale!

Aïda.

E in suo potere io sto!... Io d'Amonasro
Figlia!...

Amonasro.

In poter di lei!... No!... se lo brami
La possente rival tu vincerai,
E patria, è trono, e amor, tutto avrai.
Rivedrai le foreste imbalsamate,
Le fresche valli, i nostri templi d'ôr...

Aïda   (con trasporto).

Rivedrò le foreste imbalsamate...
Le nostre valli... i nostri templii d'ôr!

Amonasro.

Sposa felice a lui che amasti tanto,
Tripudii immensi ivi potrai gioir...

Aïda   (con trasporto)

Un'giorno solo di sì dolce incanto.
Un'ora di tal gaudio. . e poi morir!

Amonasro.

Pur rammenti che a noi l'Egizio immite,
Le case, i tempii e l'are profanò. .
Trasse in ceppi le vergini rapite. .
Madri, vecchi e fanciulli ei trucidè.

Aïda.

Ah! ben rammento quegli infausti giorni
Rammento i lutti che il mio cor soffrì. .
Deh! fate o Numi che per noi ritorni
L'alba invocata dei sereni dì.

Amonasro.

Non fia che tardi—In armi ora si desta
Il popol nostro—tutto e pronto già. .

Victory we shall have. It only remains for me to know
What path the enemy will follow.

Aïda.

Who will be able to discover it? Who?

Amonasro.

Thyself!

Aïda.

I?

Amonasro.

Radames will come here soon—he loves thee—
He leads the Egyptians. Dost thou understand?

Aïda.

Horror!
What dost thou counsel me? No, no! Never!

Amonasro   (with savage fury).

Up, then! Rise,
Egyptian legions!
With fire destroy
Our cities—
Spread terror,
Carnage and death.
To your fury
There is no longer check.

Aïda.

Ah, father!

Amonasro   (repulsing her).

My daughter
Dost thou call thyself?

Aïda   (terrified and beseeching).

Pity!

Amonasro.

Rivers of blood pour
On the cities of the vanquished—
Seest thou?—From the black gulfs
The dead are raised—
To thee they point and cry:
"For thee the country dies."

Aïda.

Pity!

Amonasro.

A horrible ghost
Among the shadows to us approaches—

Vittoria avrem..Solo a saper mi resta
Qual sentier il nemico seguirà..

Aïda.

Chi scoprirlo potria? chi mai?

Amonasro.

Tu stessa!

Aïda.

Io!..

Amonasro.

Radamès so che qui attendi.. Ei t'ama..
Ei conduce gli Egizii.. Intendi?

Aïda.

Orrore!
Che mi consigli tu? No, no, giammai!

Amonasro   (con impeto selvaggio).

Su, dunque! sorgete
Egizie coorti!
Col fuoco struggete
Le nostre città..
Spargete il terrore,
Le stragi' le morti..
Al vostro furore
Più freno non v'ha.

Aïda.

Ah padre!

Amonasro   (respingendola).

Mia figlia
Ti chiami!..

Aïda   (atterrita e supplichevole).

Pietà!

Amonasro.

Flutti di sangue scorrono
Sulle città dei vinti..
Vedi?..dai negri vortici
Si levano gli estinti..
Ti additan essi e gridano:
"Per te la patria muor."

Aïda.

Pietà!..

Amonastro.

Una larva orribile
Fra l'ombre a moi s'affaccia..

Tremble! the fleshless arms Over thy head it raised— It is thy mother—recognize her— She curses thee.	Trema! le scarne braccia Sul capo tuo levò.. Tua madre ell'è..ravvisala.. Ti maledice..

Aïda   (in the greatest terror).
> Ah, no!
> Father.

Aïda   (nel massimo terrore).
> Ah, no!..
> Padre.

Amonasro   (repulsing her).
> Go, unworthy one! Thou'rt not my off-
>   spring—
> Thou art the slave of the Pharaohs!

Amonasro   (respingendola).
> Va, indegna! non sei mia figlia!
> Dei Faraoni tu sei la schiava.

Aïda.
> Father, their slave I am not—
> Reproach me not—curse me not;
> Thy daughter again thou canst call me—
> Of my country I will be worthy.

Aïda.
> Padre, a costoro schiava io non sono..
> Non maledirmi.. non imprecarmi..
> Tua figlia ancora potrai chiamarmi..
> Della mia patria degna sarò.

Amonasro.
> Think that a people conquered, torn to
>   pieces,
> Through thee alone can arise—

Amonasro.
> Pensa che un popolo, vinto, straziato
> Per te soltanto risorger può..

Aïda.
> O my country, O my country—how much
>   thou costest me!

Aïda.
> O patria! o patria.. quanto mi costi!

Amonasro.
> Courage! he comes—there I shall hear all.
> (Conceals himself among the palm trees.)
>   (Enter RADAMES.)

Amonasro.
> Corraggio! ei giunge.. là tutto udrò..
> (Si nasconde fra i palmizii.)
>   (RADAMES e AÏDA.)

Radames.
> I see thee again, my sweet Aïda.

Radames.
> Pur ti riveggo, mia dolce Aïda...

Aïda.
> Stop! begone. What, hopest thou still?

Aïda.
> Ti arresta, vanne... che speri ancor?

Radames.
> Love guided me to thee.

Radames.
> A te dappresso l'amor mi guida.

Aïda.
> The rites of another love await thee,
> Spouse of Amneris.

Aïda.
> Te i riti attendono d'un altro amor.
> D'Amneris sposo...

Radames.
> What sayest thou?
> Thee alone, Aïda, must I love.
> Hear me, gods!—Thou shalt be mine!

Radames.
> Che parli mai?
> Te sola, Aïda, te deggio amar.
> Gli Dei mi ascoltano... tu mia sarsi...

Aïda.
> Stain not thyself with perjury.
> Valiant I loved thee; foresworn I should not
>   love thee.

Aïda.
> D'uno spergiuro non ti machiar?
> Prode t'amai, non t'amerei spergiuro.

Radames.
> Doubtest thou my love, Aïda?

Radames.
> Dell' amor mio dubiti, Aïda?

Aïda.

　And how

　Hopest thou to free thyself from the love of
　　Amneris,

　From the King's will, from the vows of thy
　　people,

　From the wrath of the priests?

Radames.

　Hear me, Aïda.

　To the fierce pant of a new war

　The land of Ethiopia has re-awakened—

　Thy people already invade our country.

　I shall be leader of the Egyptians.

　Amid the fame, the applause of victory,

　I prostrate myself before the King, I unveil
　　to him my heart.

　Thou shalt be the reward of my glory,

　We shall live blessed by eternal love.

Aïda.

　Nor fearest thou Amneris and

　Her vindictive fury? Her revenge,

　Like a dreadful thunderbolt,

　Will fall on me, on my father, on all.

Radames.

　I protect thee.

Aïda.

　In vain! Thou couldst not—

　Still—if thou lovest me—again a way

　Of escape opens to us.

Radames.

　Which?

Aïda.

　To fly!

Radames.

　To fly!

Aïda.

　E come

　Speri sottrarti d'Amneris ai vezzi,

　Del Re al voler, del tuo popolo ai voti,

　Dei sacerdoti all' ira?

Radames.

　Odimi, Aïda.

　Nel fiero anelito di nuova guerra

　Il suolo Etiope si ridestò...

　I tuoi già invadono la nostra terra,

　Io degli Egizii duce sarò.

　Fra il suon, fra i plausi della vittoria,

　Al re mi prostro, gli svelo il cor...

　Sarai tu il serto della mia gloria,

　Vivrem beati d'eterno amor.

Aïda.

　Nè d'Amneris paventi

　Il vindice furor? la sua vendetta,

　Come folgor tremenda

　Cadrà su me, sul padre mio, su tutti.

Radames.

　Io vi difendo.

Aïda.

　Invan tu nol potresti..

　Pur... se tu m'ami... ancor s'apre una via

　Di scampo a noi...

Radames.

　Quale?

Aïda.

　Fuggire...

Radames.

　Fuggire!

FUGGIAM GLI ARDORI—*AH! FLY WITH ME* Duet (Aïda and Radames)

Andantino　　*mf* AIDA

Fug-giam gli ar-do-ri i-nos-pi-ti　　Di que-ste lan-de i-gnu-da;
Ah! fly　with me, and leave　be-hind　These des-erts bare and blight-ed;

U - na no-vel-la pa-tri-a,   al   no-stro a-mor si schiu-de.

Some coun-try, new and fresh to find, Where we may love u-nit-ed.

Là - tra fo-re-ste ver-gi-ni,   Di fio-ri pro-fu - ma-te, in

There 'mid the vir-gin for-est groves, By fair and sweet flow'rs scent-ed, In

e-sta-si be - a-te la ter-ra scor-de-rem, in e - sta-si,

qui-et joy con-tent-ed, The world will we for-get, in qui - et joy,—

_ in e - - - sta-si la__ ter - - - ra__scor-de-

— in qui - - et__ joy, The__ world_____ will__ we for-

RADAMES

rem, So-vra u-na ter-ra e-stra-nia te-co fug-gir do-vrei! ab-ban-do-nar la

get, To some strange land far dis-tant Must I then with you fly! Our home and coun-try

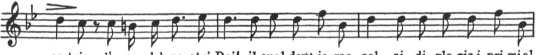

pa-tria l'a-re de' no-stri Dei! il suol dov' io rac-col-si di glo-ria i pri-mi al

leav-ing, Our gods and al-tars high! The soil where first I gath-er'd The bays that deeds re-

lo - ri; il ciel de no-stri a-mo - ri   co-me scor-dar po - trem?

quit-ed, The sky our love that light-ed, How can we e'er for-get?

AIDA

Là tra for-es-ti ver-gi-ni, di fio-ri pro-fu-ma-te, in
There 'neath the vir-gin for-est groves; By fair and sweet flow'rs scent-ed, In

e-sta-si be-a-te la ter-ra scor-de-rem, in e-
qui-et joy con-tent-ed The world will we for-get, In qui-

-sta-si,— in è-sta-si la— ter—-ra scor-de-
-et joy,— in qui-et joy The— world———— will we for-

RADAMES   AIDA

rem   Il ciel di nos-tri a-mo-ri co-me scor-dar po-trem? Sott'o il mio ciel, più
get,   The sky our love that light-ed, How can we e'er for-get? Be-neath my sky more

li-be-re là-mor ne fia con-ces-sò, ·i-vi nel tem-pio i
light and free Love's gen-'rous aid con-fid-ing; In tem-ples there a-

stes-so gli stes-si Nu-mi a-vrem, i-vi nel tem-pio i
bid-ing, Gods like your own we'll find, In tem-ples there a-

stes-so gli stes-si Nu-mi a-vrem; I-vi nel tem-pio i
bid-ing, The self-same gods we'll find, In tem-ples there a-

stes-so gli stes-si Nu-mi a-vrem; fug-giam, fug-giam!———
bid-ing the self-same gods we'll find, then fly! ah! fly!———

Radames   (hesitating).
    Aïda!
Aïda.
    Thou lovest me not—go!
Radames.
    I love thee not?
    Never mortal, nor god,
    Burnt with love so powerful as mine!
Aïda.
    Go, go! Amneris awaits thee
    At the altar.
Radames.
    No, never!
Aïda.
    Never, saidst thou?
    Then falls the axe
    On me, on my father.
Radames.
    Ah, no, let us fly!
          (With impassioned resolution.)
    Yes; let us fly from these walls,
    To the desert let us fly together;
    Here misfortune reigns alone.
    There opens to us a heaven of love.
    The boundless deserts
    Shall be our nuptial couch,
    On us the stars will shine
    With a more limpid effulgence.
Aïda.
    In the happy land
    Of my fathers heaven awaits us;
    There the air is perfumed,
    There the ground is fragrant with flowers.
    Fresh valleys and green fields
    Shall be our nuptial couch,
    On us the stars will shine
    With a more limpid effulgence.
Aïda and Radames.
    Come with me—together let us fly
    This land of grief.
    Come with me—I love thee, I love thee!
    Love shall be our leader.
              (They go rapidly aside.)
Aïda   (stopping suddenly).
    But tell me by what road
    Shall we avoid the armed hosts?

Radames   (esitante).
    Aïda!
Aïda.
    Tu non m'ami... Va!—
Radames.
    Non t'amo!
    Mortal giammi nè Dio
    Arse d'amore al par del mio possente.
Aïda.
    Va... va... ti attende all' ara
    Amneris...
Radames.
    No!... giammai!...
Aïda.
    Giammai, dicesti?
    Allor piombi la scure
    Su me, sul padre mio...
Radames.
    Ah no! fuggiamo!
          (Con appassionata risoluzione.)
    Sì: fuggiamo da queste mura,
    Al deserto insiem fuggiamo;
    Qui sol regna la sventura,
    Là si schiude un ciel d'amor.
    I deserti interminati
    A noi talamo saranno,
    Su noi gli astri brilleranno.
    Di più limpido fulgor.
Aïda.
    Nella terra avventurata
    De' miei padri, il ciel ne attende;
    Ivi l'aura è imbalsamata,
    Ivi il suolo è aromi e fior.
    Fresche valli e verdi prati
    A noi talamo saranno,
    Su noi gli astri brilleranno.
    Di più limpido fulgor.
Aïda e Radames.
    Vieni meco—insiem fuggiamo
    Questa terra di dolor—
    Vieni meco—io t'amo, io t'amo!
    A noi duce fia l'amor!
              (Si allontanano rapidamente.)
Aïda   (arrestandosi all' improvviso).
    Ma, dimmi; per qual via
    Eviterem le schiere
    Degli armati?

Radames.

The path chosen by our troops
To fall on the enemy will be deserted
Until to-morrow.

Aïda.

And that path?

Radames.

The Pass
Of Napata.

(Enter AMONASRO.)

Amonasro.

The Pass of Napata!
There shall be my people.

Radames.

Oh! who hears us?

Amonasro.

The father of Aïda and King of the Ethiopians.

Radames

(greatly agitated).

Thou, Amonasro! Thou, the King! Gods,
    what said I?
No! It is not true!—I dream—this is dilirium.

Aïda.

Ah, no! calm thyself—listen to me,
Trust thyself in my love.

Amonasro.

Aïda's love shall raise thee
To a throne.

Radames.

For thee to betray my country!
I am dishonored.

Amonasro.

No; Thou art not guilty—
It was the will of fate.
Come; beyond the Nile await us
The brave men devoted to us;
There the vows of thy heart
Shall be crowned with love.

(Enter AMNERIS from the Temple, then RAMPHIS, PRIESTS
and GUARDS.)

Amneris.

Traitor!

Aïda.

My rival!

Radames.

Il sentier scelto dai nostri
A piombar sul nemico fia deserto
Fino a domani...

Aïda.

E quel sentier?...

Radames.

Le gole
Di Nàpata?

(AMONASRO e AÏDA e RADAMES.)

Amonasro.

Di Nàpata le gole!
Ivi saranno i miei...

Radames.

Oh! chi ci ascolta?

Amonasro.

D'Aida il padre e degli Etiopi il Re.

Radames

(agitatissimo).

Tu! Amonasro!... Tu il Re?
Numi! che dissi?
No!..non è ver!..sogno... delirio è questo..

Aïda.

Ah, no! ti calma..ascoltami,
All' amor mio t'affida.

Amonasro.

A te l'amor d'Aïda
Un soglio innalzerà!

Radames.

Per te tradii la patria!
Io son disonorato..

Amonasro.

No: tu non sei colpevole—
Era voler del fato.
Vieni: oltra il Nil ne attendono
I prodi a noi devoti,
Là del tuo core i voti
Coronerà l'amor.

(AMNERIS, dal tempio, indi RAMFIS, SACERDOTI, GUARDIE e
detti.)

Amneris.

Traditor!

Aïda.

La mia rivale!..

Amonasro

  (rushing upon AMNERIS with a dagger).

Comest thou to destroy my work?
Die!

Radames (interposing himself).

 Stop, madman!

Amonasro.

 Oh, fury!

Ramphis.

 Guards, hither!

Radames (to AÏDA and AMONASRO).

 Haste!—fly!

Amonasro (drawing AÏDA away).

 Come, O daughter!

Ramphis (to the GUARDS).

 Follow them!

Radames (to RAMPHIS).

 Priest, I remain with thee.

  END OF THE THIRD ACT.

ACT IV.

SCENE I.

 Hall in the King's Palace; to the left a grand gate, which opens on the subterranean hall of judgment; passage to the right which leads to the prison of RADAMES.

Amneris

  (in a sad attitude before the gate of the hall).

My abhorred rival escapes me—
Radames awaits from the priests
The punishment of a traitor. Traitor
He is not, though he revealed
The high secret of war. He wished to fly—
To fly with her—traitors all!
To death, to death! Oh, what did I say? I
 love him—
I love him always—desperate, mad
Is this love which destroys my life.
Oh! if he could love me!
I would save him—and how?
Let me try. Guards: Radames comes.

  (Enter RADAMES, guarded.)

Amneris.

 Already the priests assemble,
 Arbiters of thy fate;
 Of the horrible crime however

Amonasro

  (avventandosi ad AMNERIS con un pugnale).

Vieni a strugger l'opre mia!
Muori!

Radames (frapponendosi).

 Arresta, insano!..

Amonasro.

 Oh rabbia!

Ramfis.

 Guardie, olà.

Radames (ad AÏDA e AMONASRO)

 Presto! fuggite!..

Amonasro (trascinando AÏDA).

 Vieni, o figlia!..

Ramfis (alle GUARDIE).

 Li inseguite!

Radames (a RAMFIS).

 Sacerdote, io resto a te.

  FINE DELL' ATTO TERZO.

ATTO IV.

SCENA I

 Sala nel Palazzo del Re. Alla sinistra, una gran porta che mette alla sala sotterranea della sentenze.—Andito destra che conduce alla prigione di RADAMES.

Amneris

  (mestamente atteggiata davanti la porta del sotterraneo).

L'abborrita rivale a me sfuggia..
Dai sacerdoti Radamès attende
Dei traditor la pena,—Traditore
Egli non è.. Pur rivelò di guerra
L'alto segreto..egli fuggir volea..
Con lei fuggire.. Traditori tutti!
A morte! A morte!..Oh! che mai parlo
 Io l'amo,
Io l'amo sempre..Disperato, insano
E quest' amor che la mia vita strugge.
Oh! s'ei potesse amarmi!..
Vorrei salvarlo.. E come?
Si tenti!.. Guardie: Radamès qui venga.

  (RADAMES condotto dalle guardie, e AMNERIS.)

Amneris.

 Già i sacerdoti adunansi
 Arbitri del tuo fato;
 Pur della accusa orribile

Still it is given thee to exculpate thyself.
Exculpate thyself, and grace for thee
I will beg from the throne;
And a messenger of pardon—
Of life, to thee I will be.

Radames.

Of my exculpation the judges
Will never hear the sound.
Before gods and men
Neither vile nor guilty do I feel.
My incautious lips
Uttered the fatal secret, it is true,
But pure my thought
And my honor remained.

Amneris.

Then save and exculpate thyself.

Radames.

No.

Amneris.

Thou wilt die.

Radames.

Life
I abhor; the font
Of every joy dried up,
Every hope vanished,
I wish only to die.

Amneris.

To die! Ah; thou shouldst live!
Yes, for my love thou shalt live;
For thee I have undergone
The dreadful anguish of death.
I loved thee—I suffered so much—
I watched through the nights in tears.
Country and throne and life—
All I would give for thee.

Radames.

For her I too betrayed
The country and my honor.

Amneris.

Of her no more——

Radames.

Infamy
Awaits me, and thou wishest that I live?
Utterly wretched thou madest me;
Aïda thou hast taken from me;

Scolparti ancor ti è dato:
Ti scolpa, e la tua grazia
Io pregherò dal trono,
E nunzia di perdono,
Di vita, a te sarò.

Radames.

Di mie discolpe i giudici
Mai non udran l'accento;
Dinanzi ai Numi e agli uomini
Nè vil, nè reo mi sento.
Profferse il labbro incauto
Fatal segreto, è vero,
Ma puro il mio pensiero
E 'l onore mio restò.

Amneris.

Salvati dunque e scolpati.

Radames.

No.

Amneris.

Tu morrai. .

Radames.

La vita
Abhorro; d'ogni gaudio
La fonte inaridita,
Svanita ogni speranza,
Sol bramo di morir.

Amneris.

Morire!..ah!..tu dei vivere!..
Si, all' amor mio vivrai;
Per te le angoscie orribili
Di morte io già provai;
T'amai. .soffersi tanto. .
Vegliai le notti in pianto..
E patria, e trono, e vita
Tutto darei per te.

Radames.

Per essa anch' io la patria
E l'onor mio tradiva...

Amneris.

Di lei non più!...

Radames.

L'infamia
Mi attende e vuoi che io viva?...
Misero appien mi festi,
Aïda a me togliesti,

Killed her perhaps!   And for gift
Thou offerest life to me?

Amneris.

I—the cause of her death?
No!   Aïda lives!

Radames.

Lives?

Amneris.

In the desperate struggle
Of the fugitive hordes
Fell her father alone——

Radames.

And she?——

Amneris.

She disappeared, nor more news
Had we.

Radames.

May the gods lead her
Safe to her native walls,
And let her not know the unhappy fate
Of him who will die for her.

Amneris.

Now, if I save thee, swear to me
That thou wilt not see her more.

Radames.

I cannot do it!

Amneris.

Renounce her
Forever, and thou shalt live!

Radames.

I cannot do it!

Amneris.

Yet, once more;
Renounce her!

Radames.

It is in vain!

Amneris.

Wouldst thou die, then, madman?

Radames.

I am ready to die.

Amneris.

Who saves thee, O wretch,
From the fate that awaits thee?
To fury hast thou changed
A love that had no equal.

Spenta l' hai forse... e in dono
Offri la vita a me?

Amneris.

Io...di sua morte origine!
No!... vive Aïda...

Radames.

Vive!

Amneris.

Nei disperati aneliti
Dell' orde fuggitive
Sol cadde il padre..

Radames.

Ed ella?

Amneris.

Sparve, nè più novella
S'ebbe...

Radames.

Gli Dei l'adducano
Salve alle patrie mura,
E ignori la sventura
Di chi per lei morrà!

Amneris.

Or, s'io ti salvo, giurami
Che più non la vedrai...

Radames.

Nol posso!

Amneris.

A lei rinunzia
Per sempre...e tu vivrai!...

Radames.

Nol posso!

Amneris.

Anco una volta
A lei rinunzia..

Radames.

E vano..

Amneris.

Morir vuoi dunque, insano?

Radames.

Pronto a morir son già.

Amneris.

Chi ti salva, o sciagurato,
Dalla sorte che ti aspetta?
In furore hai tu cangiato
Un amor ch' equel non ha.

Revenge for my tears
Heaven will now consummate.

Radames.

Death is a supreme blessing,
If for her it is given me to die;
In undergoing the last extremity
My heart will feel great joy.
Human anger I fear no more,
I fear only thy pity.

(Exit RADAMES, surrounded by Guards.)

Amneris (falls desolate on a seat).

Ah me! I feel myself dying. Oh! who will save him?
And in their power
I myself threw him. Now I curse thee,
Atrocious jealousy, who didst cause his death
And the eternal grief of my heart!

(Turns and sees the PRIESTS, who cross the stage to enter the subterranean hall.)

What do I see? Behold the fatal,
The merciless ministers of death!
Oh, that I might not see those white ghosts!

(Covers her face in her hands.)

Priests (in the subterranean hall).

Spirit of the gods descend upon us!
Awaken us to the ray of thy eternal light:
By our lips make thy justice known.

Amneris.

Gods, pity my torn heart.
He is innocent; save him, O gods!
Desperate, tremendous is my sorrow!

(RADAMES, between Guards, crosses the stage and descends the subterranean hall—AMNERIS on seeing him utters a cry.)

Ramphis (in the subterranean hall).

Radames, Radames: thou didst reveal
The country's secrets to the foreigner.

Priests.

Defend thyself!

Ramphis.

He is silent.

All.

Traitor!

Ramphis.

Radames, Radames: thou didst desert
From the camp the day preceding the battle.

De'miei pianti la vendetta
Ora il cielo compirà.

Radames.

E la morte un ben supremo
Se per lei morir m' è dato:
Nel subir l'estremo fato
Gaudii immensi il core avrà;
L'ira umana io più non temo,
Temo sol la tua pietà.

(RADAMES parte circondato dalle Guardie.)

Amneris (cade desolata su un sedile).

Ohimè!..Morir mi sento.. Oh! chi lo salva?
E in poter di costoro
Io stessa lo gettai!...Ora, a te impreco
Atroce gelosia, che la sua morte
E il lutto eterno del mio cor segnasti!

(Si volge e vede i SACERDOTI che attraversano la scena per entrare nel sotterraneo.)

Che veggo! Ecco i fatali
Gli inesorati ministri di morte...
Oh! ch' io non veggo quelle bianche larve!

(Si copre il volto colle mani.)

Sacerdoti (nel sotterraneo).

Spirito de l'Nume sovra noi discendi!
Ne avviva al raggio dell' eterna luce;
Pel labbro nostro tua giustizia apprendi.

Amneris.

Numi, pietà del mio straziato core...
Egli è innocente, lo salvate, o Numi!
Disperato, tremendo è il mio dolore!

(RADAMES, fra le Guardie, attraversa la scena e scende nel sotterraneo—AMNERIS al vederlo, mette un grido.)

Ramfis (nel sotterraneo).

Radamès—Radamès: tu rivelasti
Della patria i segretti allo straniero...

Sacerdoti.

Discólpati!

Ramfis.

Egli tace..

Tutti.

Traditor!

Ramfis.

Radamès, Radamès: tu disertasti
Dal campo il dì che precedea la pugna.

Priests.

Defend thyself!

Ramphis.

He is silent.

All.

Traitor!

Ramphis.

Radames, Radames: thou brokest thy faith,
Foresworn to thy country, king and honor.

Priests.

Defend thyself!

Ramphis.

He is silent.

All.

Traitor!
Radames thy fate is decided:
Thou shalt die the death of the infamous.
Under the altar of the angered god
To thee alive be opened the tomb.

Amneris.

To him alive—the tomb! Oh the infamous
    wretches!
Never satisfied with blood:
And then call themselves ministers of
    heaven!
(Attacking the PRIESTS, who issue from the subterranean
hall.)
Priests, you have done a wicked deed—
Infamous tigers! thirsting for blood;
You outrage earth and gods.
You punish him who has done no wrong.

Priests.

He is a traitor! he shall die.

Amneris
                    (to RAMPHIS).
Priest, this man whom thou slayest—
Thou knowest it—was loved by me.
The curse of a broken heart,
With his blood, will recoil on thee!

Priests.

He is a traitor! He shall die!
                (They withdraw slowly.)

Amneris.

Impious band—anathema! On you
The vengeance of heaven will fall!
            (Exit in despair.)

Sacerdoti.

Discólpati!

Ramfis.

Egli tace..

Tutti.

Traditor!

Ramfis.

Radamès, Radamès: tua fè violasti,
Alla patria spergiuro, al Re, all' onor.

Sacerdoti.

Discólpati!

Ramfis.

Egli tace..

Tutti.

Traditor!
Radamès è deciso il tuo fato;
Degli infami la morte tu avrai;
Sotto l'ara del Nume sdegnato
A te vivo fia schiuso l'avel.

Amneris.

A lui vivo..la tomba..Oh! gli infami!
Nè di sangue son paghi giammai..
E si chiaman ministri del ciel!
(Investendo i SACERDOTI che escono die sotterraneo.)
Sacerdoti: compiste un delitto..
Tigri infami di sangue assetate..
Voi le terra ed i Numi eltraggiate..
Voi punite chi colpa non ha.

Sacerdoti.

E traditor! morrà.

Amneris
                    (a RAMFIS).
Sacerdote! quest' uomo che uccidi,
Tu io sai.. da me un giorno fu amato..
L'anatéma d'un core straziato
Col suo sangue su te ricardrà!

Sacerdoti.

E traditor! morrà.
                (Si allontanano lentamente.)

Amneris.

Empia razza! anatéma! su voi!
La vendetta del ciel scenderà!
            (Esce disperata.)

20

SCENE II.

The Scene is divided into two floors. The upper floor represents the Interior of the Temple of Vulcan, resplendent with light and gold; the lower floor a subterranean hall; long rows of arcades which are lost in the darkness; colossal statue of Osiris, with the hands crossed, sustains the pilasters of the vault.

RADAMES is in the subterranean hall, on the steps of the staircase by which he has descended; above, two PRIESTS, engaged in closing the stone over the subterranean entrance.

Radames.

The fatal stone is closed above me—
Behold my tomb. The light of day
I shall see no more. I shall no more see
   Aïda.
Aïda, where art thou? May thou at least
Live happy, and my dreadful fate
Never know. What a groan! A ghost!
A vision—No, it is a human shape—
Heavens! Aïda!

Aïda.

It is I.

Radames.

Thou—in this tomb?

Aïda.

My heart, prophetic of thy sentence,
Into this tomb which opened itself for thee
I furtive made my way.
And here afar from every human glance
In thy arms I wished to die.

Radames.

To die! So pure and beautiful!
To die for love of me;
In the flower of thy youth
To fly from life!
Heaven created thee for love,
And I kill thee by having loved thee!
No, thou shalt not die!
Too much I loved thee—
Too beautiful art thou.

Aïda
    (raving).

Seest thou the angel of death
Radiant to us approaches?
He takes us to eternal joys
Under his golden pinions.
Above us heaven has already opened;
There every grief ceases;

SCENA II.

La Scena è divisa in due piani. Il piano superiore rappresenta l'interno del Tempio di Vulcano splendente d'oro e di luce; il piano inferiore un sotterraneo. Lunghe file d'arcate si perdono nell' oscurità. Statue colossali d'Osiride colle mani incrociate sostengono i pilastri della volta.

RADAMES è nel sotterraneo sui gradini della scala per cui è disceso—Al di sopra, due SACERDOTI intenti a chiudere la pietra del sotterraneo.

Radames.

La fatal pietra sovra me si chiuse..
Ecco la tomba mia.—Del dì la luce
Più non vedrò..Non rivedò più Aïda...
—Aïda, ove sei tu? Possa tu almeno
Viver felice e la mia sorte orrenda
Sempre ignorar!—Qual gemito!—Una
   larva..
Una vision..No; forma umana è questa..
Cielo!..Aïda!

Aïda.

Son io..

Radames.

Tu.. in questa tomba!

Aïda.

Presago il core della tua condanna,
In questa tomba che per te si apriva
Io penetrai furtiva..
E qui lontana da ogni umano sguardo
Nelle tue braccia desiair morire.

Radames.

Morir! si pura e bella!
Morir per me d'amore..
Degli anni tuoi nel fiore
Fuggir la vita!
T'aveva il cielo per l'amor creata,
Ed io t'uccido per averti amata!
No, non morrai!
Troppo io t'amai!..
Troppo sei bella!..

Aïda
    (vaneggiando).

Vedi?..di morte l'angelo
Radiante a noi si appressa..
Ne adduce a eterni gaudii
Sovra i suoi vanni d'ôr.
Su noi già il ciel dischiudersi..
Ivi ogni affanno cessa..

There begins the ecstasy

Of an immortal love.

(Songs and dances of the Priestesses in the Temple.)

Aïda.

Sad song!

Radames.

The jubilee

Of the priests!

Aïda.

Our hymn of death . . . .

Radames

(trying to move the stone of the vault).

My strong arms

Cannot move thee, O fatal stone!

Aïda.

It is vain—all is over

For us on earth.

Radames

(with desperate resignation).

It is true—it is true!

(Goes to Aïda and supports her.)

Aïda and Radames.

O earth, farewell! Farewell, vale of

tears—

Dream of joy which vanished in grief.

Heaven opens itself to us, and the wandering souls

Fly to the rays of eternal day.

(Aïda falls gently into the arms of Radames.)

(Amneris in mourning robes appears in the temple, and goes to prostrate herself on the stone which closes the vault.)

Amneris.

Peace I pray for thee, O adored corse;

Isis appeased, may she unclose heaven to thee!

Ivi comincia l'estasi

D'un immortale amor.

(Canti e danze della Sacerdotesse nel Tempio.)

Aïda.

Triste canto!..

Radames.

Il tripudio

Dei Sacerdoti..

Aïda.

Il nostro inno di morte..

Radames

(cercando di smuovere la pietra del sotterraneo).

Nè le mie forti braccia

Smuovere ti potranno o fatal pietra!

Aïda.

Invan!..tutto è finito

Sulla terra per noi..

Radames

(con desolata rassegnazione).

E vero! è vero!

(Si avvicina ad Aïda e la sorrege.)

Aïda e Radames.

O terra, addio; addio valle di pianti..

Sogno di gaudio che in dolor svani..

A noi si schiude il cielo, e l'alme erranti

Volano al raggio dell' eterno di.

(Aïda cade dolcemente fra le braccia di Radames.)

(Amneris in abito di lutto apparisce nel Tempio e va a prostrarsi sulla pietra che chiude il sotterraneo.)

Amneris.

Pace t'imploro—salma adorata..

Isi placata—ti schiuda il ciel!

THE END.

Lightning Source UK Ltd.
Milton Keynes UK
UKOW07f1807150315

247912UK00004B/234/P